The world's best JOKES for kids
VOLUME 1

Every single one illustrated

SWERLING + LAZAR

Andrews McMeel
PUBLISHING®

This book is for

Gabriel + Jamie   Siena + Dash

and all the other
joke-tellers out there,
young and old.

DANGER!

This book contains a lot of silly, corny, brilliant, and funny **JOKES!**

What is heavy and
wears glass slippers?

Cinderelephant.

What did the headteacher say
to the misbehaving egg?

You're egg-spelled!

Which is the most magical dog?

A labracadabrador.

What do you call a bear with no ears?

B.

You can tune a guitar.

But you can't tuna fish.

What do you call
a bee that comes
from America?

 USB.

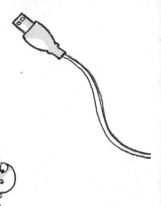

Why can't you give
Elsa a balloon?

 Because she'll
let it go.

What do you call an elephant that doesn't matter?

An irrelephant.

What did the buffalo say when he dropped his son off at school?

Bison.

What do you call an ant that won't go away?

Permanant.

Why was the king only 12 inches tall?

Because he was a ruler.

How do you describe a person with no body and just a nose?

Nobody nose.

I was wondering, why does a frisbee appear larger the closer it gets?

Then it hit me.

What do you call the new girl at the bank?

The nutella.

Did you hear about the hungry clock?

It went back four seconds.

Why do seagulls fly over the sea and not the bay?

Because otherwise they'd be bagels.

Why are pirates called pirates?

Because they arrrrrrr.

What do you call having your granny on speed dial?

Instagran.

What happened to the dog that swallowed a firefly?

It barked with de-light!

What treat is never on time?

Choco-late.

What do you call a bear with no teeth?

A gummy bear.

What is E.T. short for?

Because he's got such little legs.

Why did the robber take a bath?

He wanted to make a clean getaway.

How do you make an octopus laugh?

With ten-tickles.

What do you call a nervous javelin thrower?

Shakespeare.

Where do crayons go on vacation?

Color-ado.

What do you call a belt with a clock on it?

A waist of time.

Why did the giraffe get bad grades?

She always had her head in the clouds.

Have you ever tried to eat a clock?

It's very time consuming.

What did the blanket say to the bed?

"Don't worry, I've got you covered."

What did the one snail say to the other?

"It's about slime we started dating."

What do you call a positive bunny?

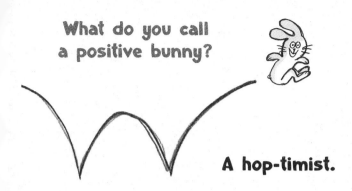

A hop-timist.

What kind of math do birds like?

Owlgebra.

What do sea monsters eat?

Fish & ships.

Why did the horse keep falling over?

He just wasn't stable.

Why did the traffic light turn red?

You would too if you had to change on the side of the road.

I've just returned from a once-in-a-lifetime vacation.

Never again.

Why was six scared of seven?

Because seven ate nine.

I hate Russian dolls.

So full of themselves.

What's the best thing about Switzerland?

I don't know, but their flag is a huge plus.

What did the one fish say to the other?

"Hey, long time no sea."

Why did the tomato blush?

It saw the salad dressing.

What do you give a horse with a cold?

Cough stirrup.

What did Bacon say to Tomato?

"Lettuce get together!"

Why don't skeletons fight each other?

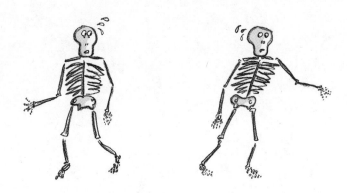

They just don't have the guts.

What do you call a line of men waiting for a haircut?

A barbeque.

What did the dad chimney say to the little chimney?

"You're too young to smoke!"

What dog keeps the best time?

A watch dog.

What did the fish say when he swam into the wall?

"Dam!"

Why was the dog feeling sorry for himself?

Because his life was so ruff.

What did the girl say when she threw the slug across the room?

"Gosh, how slime flies."

What do you get when you cross a monkey with a peach?

An ape-ricot.

What do you call a polar bear on a desert island?

Lost.

What did Mrs. Earthworm say to her son when he came home late?

"Where on earth have you been?"

What happens when you annoy a rabbit?

You have a bad hare day.

What kind of lights did Noah use on the ark?

Flood lights.

Time flies like an arrow.

Fruit flies like a banana.

What's the best kind of snack to eat during a horror movie?

I scream.

Why was the bed wearing a disguise?

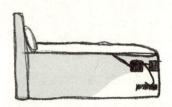

Because it was under cover.

Did you hear about the smelly fairy?

Her name was Stinkerbell.

Who brings kittens for Christmas?

Santa claws.

The teacher shouted at me for something I didn't do.

What was it?

My homework.

What did the martian say to the flower bed?

"Take me to your weeder!"

Did you hear about the actress who fell through the floor?

It was just a stage she was going through.

When do you stop on green and go on red?

When you're eating watermelon.

Who helped the monster go to the ball?

Its scary godmother.

Did you hear about the restaurant on Mars?

Great food but no atmosphere.

Why did the girl's parents scream when they saw her grades?

Because she had a bee on her report card.

Why do flamingos stand on one leg?

Because if they lifted it, they'd fall over.

How did the french fry propose to the hamburger?

He gave her an onion ring.

How do you stop a dog from barking
in the back seat of the car?

**Put him on the front
seat of the car.**

What do peanut
butter and jelly
do around the
campfire?

They tell toast stories.

What do you get when you cross
a pig with a millipede?

Bacon and legs.

What do you call a bear standing in the rain?

A drizzly bear.

What did the mother corn say to her kids?

"Don't forget to clean behind your ears."

What is the craziest way to travel?

By locomotive.

Why did the ninja spend the day in bed?

He had kung-flu.

Why did the cookie complain about being sick?

He was feeling crummy.

What is a baby's motto?

If at first you don't succeed, cry, cry again.

"You missed school yesterday."

"To tell you the truth, I didn't really miss it."

What happens if you eat yeast and shoe polish?

You'll rise and shine every morning!

What do you call an alligator in a vest?

An investigator.

What do you call a fake noodle?

An Impasta.

Where do rabbits go after their wedding?

On a bunny-moon.

Why did the little birdie fly to the hospital?

To get tweetment.

What is extremely heavy, has 6 wheels, and flies?

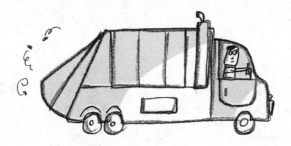

A garbage truck.

How did the snail get a view of New York City?

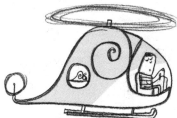

By shell-icopter.

Why did the man jump up and down before drinking his juice?

The instructions on the carton said, "Shake well before drinking."

Why did the chicken cross the mobius strip?

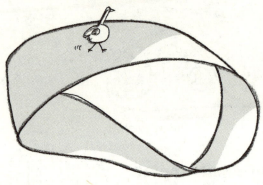

To get to the same side.

What did the tree say to the flower?

"I'm rooting for you."

Why did the man run around his bed?

Because he was trying to catch up on his sleep.

Can a flea jump higher than a bus?

Of course! Buses can't jump.

Why wouldn't the monster eat the clown?

Because he suspected it would taste funny.

Why are ghosts such bad liars?

Because you can see right through them.

Why did the math book look so sad?

It had lots of problems.

What did one wall say to the other?

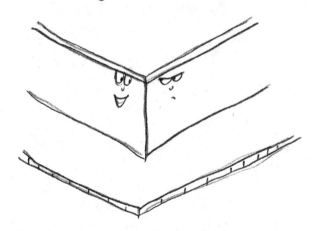

"Let's meet at the corner."

What does a raincloud wear under its clothes?

Thunderwear.

Why did the banana wear sunscreen on the beach?

He didn't want to peel.

How did the
baseball player
lose his house?

He made his
home run.

Why did the golfer wear
two pairs of pants?

In case he got a hole in one.

Why was everyone
looking up and cheering?

They were
ceiling fans.

Slept like a log
last night.

Woke up in the
fireplace.

What do you call a pig that knows karate?

A pork chop.

Did you hear about the claustrophobic astronaut?

He just needed space.

Why was the broom late for school?

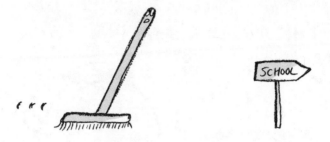

Because it over swept.

Why was the nose feeling sad?

Because it was tired of being picked on.

What nursery rhyme do camels like best?

Humpty Dumpty.

What do you call a dentist who fixes crocodiles' teeth?

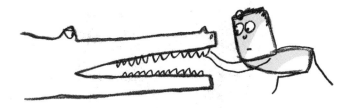

Totally crazy.

Did you hear about the teacher who was cross-eyed?

He couldn't control his pupils.

How does an Eskimo fix his broken toys?

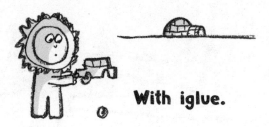

With iglue.

Why can one never take balloons seriously?

Because they're full of hot air.

Why couldn't the monster get to sleep?

Because it was afraid that there were children under the bed.

What stays in the corner yet travels across the world?

A stamp.

Why didn't the skeleton go to the ball?

Because he had no body to dance with.

What's the difference between boogers and broccoli?

Kids won't eat broccoli.

What did one flea say to the other?

Shall we hop there or take the dog?

What did the one tube of glue say to the other?

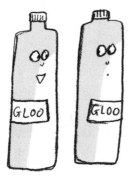

"Let's stick together."

I went to the doctor yesterday and asked if she could do anything for wind.

So she gave me a kite.

Why can't a nose be 12 inches long?

Because it would be a foot.

What do you take before every meal?

You take
your seat.

Why did the scarecrow win a medal?

Because he was outstanding in his field.

What do you get when a chicken lays its eggs on the top of a hill?

Eggrolls.

What did the cucumber say to the vinegar?

"This is a fine pickle you've got us into!"

A chicken crossing the road...

is poultry in motion.

It's difficult explaining puns to kleptomaniacs.

They always take things, literally.

Why didn't the girl trust the ocean?

Because there was something fishy about it.

What do you call a dinosaur that's worried all the time?

A nervous Rex.

Why did the girl drop the clock out the window?

Because she wanted to see time fly.

What starts with E, ends with E, and has only one letter in it?

Envelope.

What is a bat's motto?

Hang in there.

What do you get when you cross a comedian with crochet?

A knit wit.

How do cats end a fight?

They hiss and make up.

What do you call a man who rolls around in leaves?

Russell.

What's black and smells like red paint?

Black paint.

What do you call a Roman emperor when he catches a cold?

Julius Sneezer.

Where should you leave your dog when you go shopping?

In the barking lot.

What do you give an elephant with big feet?

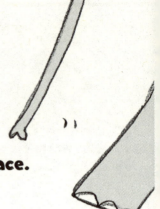

Lots of space.

What do cats call mice?

Delicious.

Why did the baker stop making donuts?

He got tired of the hole thing.

What do you get when you cross a cow with an earthquake?

A milkshake.

How do you toast a sheep?

"Here's to ewe!"

Why did the computer cross the road?

To get a byte to eat.

What do you call a robot that always takes the longest route?

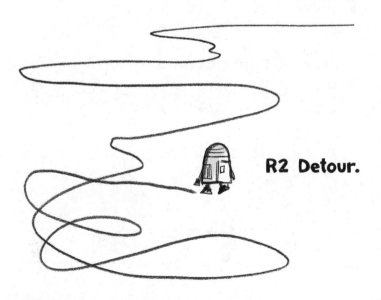

R2 Detour.

What do you call a chicken with lettuce in its eye?

Chicken caesar salad.

What did the sushi say to the bee?

WASABI!

What has one horn and gives milk?

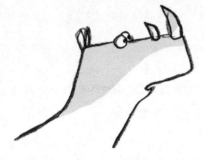

A milk truck.

How did the fisherman go deaf?

He lost his herring.

The worst part about being a birthday cake is when you're set on fire...

...and then eaten by the hero that saves you.

Why was the rabbit unhappy?

She was having a bad hare day.

What gets wetter as it dries?

A towel.

How do you catch a squirrel?

Climb a tree and act like a nut.

What did the policemen do with the hamburger?

They gave him a good grilling.

My friend keeps trying to convince me that he's a compulsive liar.

But I don't believe him.

Why did the house go to the doctor?

Because it had a window pane.

What happens to astronauts who misbehave?

They're grounded.

On the other hand...

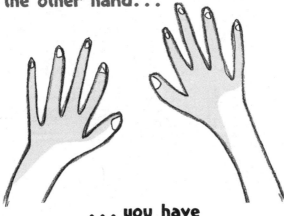

...you have different fingers.

This is my step ladder.

I never knew my biological ladder.

Don't you hate it when someone answers their own questions?

I do.

I told my doctor that I broke my arm in two places.

She told me to stop going to those places.

Knock Knock.

Who's there?

Knock.

Knock who?

Knock Knock.

Bacon and eggs walk into
a cafe and order some sodas.

The waiter says, "Sorry,
we don't serve breakfast."

I really must get rid of
my vacuum cleaner.

It's just
gathering dust.

What do religious rabbits say before they eat?

"Lettuce pray."

Where do you find a cow with no legs?

Right where you left it.

Exaggerations went up by a million percent last year.

How do you count cows?

With a cowculator.

What do you call a boomerang that doesn't come back?

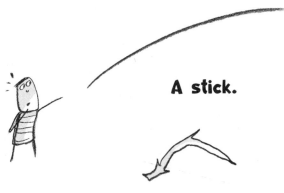

A stick.

Two antennas met on a roof, fell in love, and got married.

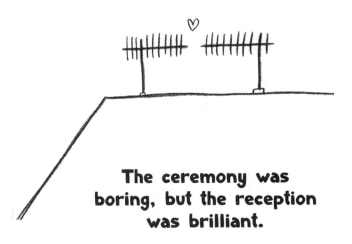

The ceremony was boring, but the reception was brilliant.

What occurs once in a minute, twice in a moment, but never in a decade?

The letter "m."

The grammar teacher was very logical.

He had a lot of comma sense.

Did you hear about the really rich rabbit?

He was a millionhare.

Why are hairdressers never late for work?

They know all the short cuts.

What is the color of the wind?

Blew.

Where does a sheep go for a haircut?

To the baaa baaa shop.

How much room is needed for fungi to grow?

As mushroom as possible.

How do you know carrots are good for your eyes?

Have you ever seen a rabbit wearing glasses?

Have you heard about corduroy pillows?

They're making headlines.

Knock knock.

Who's there?

Beats.

Beats who?

Beats me.

What's an elephant's favorite vegetable?

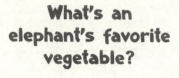

Squash.

Two penguins walk into a bar...

which is stupid, because the second one really should have seen it.

Where do cows go for entertainment?

To the moo-vies.

What do you get when you cross a parrot and a centipede?

A walkie-talkie.

Do you want to hear a bad cat joke?

Just kitten.

What is a rabbit's favorite dance style?

Hip-Hop.

What do you call a ghost's mom and dad?

Transparents.

What do you call a bear in a phone booth?

Stuck.

What does the man in the moon do when his hair gets too long?

Eclipse it!

What did the grape say when he was pinched?

Nothing, he just gave a little wine.

Did you hear about the vampire bike that went round biting people?

It was a vicious cycle.

Why was the cookie sad?

Because her mom was a wafer so long.

Why did the chicken cross the road?

To hunt somebody down.

Knock knock!

Who's there?

The chicken.

What's the difference between a weird rabbit and a sporty rabbit?

One's a bit funny, the other's a fit bunny.

What did the cat say when she lost all her money?

"I'm paw!"

"This is your captain speaking."

"AND THIS IS YOUR CAPTAIN SHOUTING."

What did one plant say to another?

"What's stomata?"

What do you call a cat that lives in an igloo?

An Eskimew.

Where do you find giant snails?

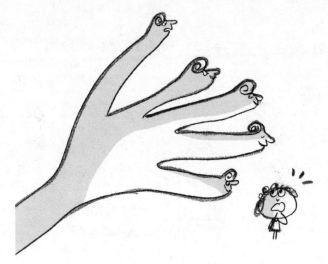

On the ends of giants' fingers.

Yesterday I held the door open for a clown.

I thought it was a nice jester.

You can always trust a glue salesman.

They tend to stick to their word.

I didn't realize my dad was a construction site thief.

But when I got home, all the signs were there.

Can February march?

No, but April may.

What starts with a P, ends with an E, and has ten thousand letters in it?

A post office.

I really wanted
a camouflage shirt...

but I couldn't find one.

"I stand corrected,"

...said the man in the
orthopedic shoes.

What swims and starts with a T?

Two ducks.

What's orange and sounds like a parrot?

A carrot.

Have I told you the deja vu joke before?

The past, present, and future
walk into a bar.

It was tense.

What did the farmer say when
he couldn't find his tractor?

"Where's my
tractor?"

How many cats can you put into an empty box?

Only one. After that, the box isn't empty.

I feel sorry for that calendar.

Its days are numbered.

What's brown and sticky?

A stick.

Why did the two fours skip lunch?

They already 8.

Why did the can crusher quit his job?

Because it was soda pressing.

How much did the pirate pay for his hook and peg?

An arm and a leg.

What do you call a crocodile with GPS?

A navi-gator.

How can you drop a raw egg onto a cement floor without cracking it?

**Any way you want.
Cement floors are very hard to crack.**

What color is a burp?

Burple.

Why did the toilet paper go downstairs?

To get to the bottom.

What side of a sheep has the most wool?

The outside.

What is heavy forward but not backward?

Ton.

Did you hear about the two bed bugs who met in the mattress?

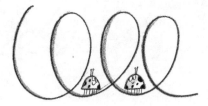

They got married in the spring.

What's the dream of
every cow?

**To go to the
mooooo-n.**

What's the difference
between roast beef
and pea soup?

You can roast beef, but you
can't pea soup.

How did the dinosaur know we were coming?

The bronto-saw-us.

What accidents happen every 24 hours?

Day breaks

and night falls.

I was struggling to figure out how lightning works.

Then it struck me.

"Nostalgia just isn't what it used to be..."

My sister and I often laugh about how competitive we are.

But I laugh more.

How did the scientist invent bug spray?

He started from scratch.

What did the bride say when she dropped her bouquet?

"Whoopsy daisies!"

What did the orange say to the banana when they were looking for the apple?

"Keep your eyes peeled."

What do you call cheese that isn't yours?

Nacho cheese.

How can you go surfing
in the kitchen?

On the microwave.

What do you get when you wake up and realize you've run out of coffee?

A depresso.

What did the sheep say to his girlfriend?

"I love ewe."

Why did the laptop get glasses?

To improve its web sight.

What was the pessimist's blood type?

B-negative.

Why couldn't the monkey catch the banana?

The banana split.

What did the one leaf say to the other?

"I'm falling for you."

How do you make a hot dog stand?

You take away its chair.

Where does a grumpy gorilla sit?

Anywhere he likes.

Why do giraffes have such long necks?

Because their feet smell.

Which word is always spelled incorrectly?

Incorrectly.

Why did the chicken cross the playground?

To get to the other slide.

What's orange and points north?

A magnetic carrot.

What do you call a dinosaur wearing a blindfold?

A doyouthinkhesaurus?

How do you get down from a camel?

You don't. You get down from a goose.

Did I tell you the gossip about the butter?

Actually, I don't think I will, as you'll probably spread it.

What did the ostrich say when it laid a square egg?

"Owwww!"

What do you get when you cross a laptop with an elephant?

Loads of memory.

What do you call a homeless snail?

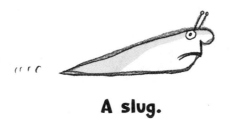

A slug.

What do you call two giraffes in a head-on collision?

A giraffic jam.

How do bananas answer the phone?

"Yellow."

What snake has the cleanest front window on its car?

The windshield viper.

How did the calendar survive on the desert island?

It ate all the dates.

What do you call spiders on honeymoon?

Newlywebs.

Why was the potato wearing socks?

To keep her pota-toes warm.

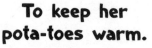

What do you call a lost wolf?

A where wolf.

What does a musician use to clean her teeth?

A tuba toothpaste.

How do monkeys stay fit?

They go to the jungle gym.

What do you call the soft tissue between a shark's teeth?

A slow swimmer.

She had a photographic memory.

But sadly she never developed it.

Why can't you hear a pterodactyl in the bathroom?

Because it has a silent pee.

Have you laughed aloud reading VOLUME 2?

The World's Best Jokes for Kids Volume 1

copyright © 2019 by Lisa Swerling and Ralph Lazar. All rights reserved.
Printed in the United States of America. No part of this book may be used
or reproduced in any manner whatsoever without written permission except
in the case of reprints in the context of reviews.

Andrews McMeel Publishing
a division of Andrews McMeel Universal
1130 Walnut Street, Kansas City, Missouri 64106

www.andrewsmcmeel.com

22 23 24 25 26 VEP 10 9 8 7 6 5

ISBN: 978-1-4494-9798-9

Library of Congress Control Number: 2018952722

Made by:
Versa Press Inc.
1465 Spring Bay Road
East Peoria, Illinois 61611
5th Printing—January 3, 2022

For lots more funny, silly, and random jokes,
visit us online:
www.lastlemon.com/silliness
www.instagram.com/silliness.is
www.facebook.com/silliness.is

Send us a joke. If we like it,
we'll illustrate it:
www.lastlemon.com/silliness/submit

ATTENTION: SCHOOLS AND BUSINESSES

Andrews McMeel books are available at quantity discounts with
bulk purchase for educational, business, or sales promotional use.
For information, please e-mail the Andrews McMeel Publishing
Special Sales Department: specialsales@amuniversal.com.